T0054011

ZONDERVAN

The Weekly Purpose Project
© 2022 Zondervan

Requests for information should be addressed to:
Zondervan, 3900 Sparks Dr. SE, Grand Rapids, Michigan 49546

ISBN 978-0-310-46177-7 (audiobook)
ISBN 978-0-310-46176-0 (eBook)
ISBN 978-0-310-46172-2 (HC)

Art direction: Tiffany Forrester
Interior design: Denise Froehlich
Interior photography: Noelle Glaze
Interior art: Shutterstock.com and istockphoto.com

Printed in China

22 23 24 25 26 GRI 10 9 8 7 6 5 4 3 2 1

A gift for

....

From

....

Date

....

THE
WEEKLY
PURPOSE
PROJECT

A CHALLENGE TO
JOURNAL, REFLECT, AND
PURSUE PURPOSE

MOLLY HODGIN

Contents

Vision

How God Wants You to Help

Action

Fulfill Your Purpose

Introduction

Discovering the Purpose God Gave You

*And we know that for those who love God
all things work together for good, for those
who are called according to his purpose.*

ROMANS 8:28 ESV

Do you know your purpose? Do you wake up every morning raring to go and then go to sleep each night satisfied with what you've done that day to make the world a better place? If so, you are very fortunate to have your purpose so clear and defined. But if your purpose is still a bit of a mystery to you, then this is the book for you.

This is more than just a journal or devotional. This is a guide to help you tap into your passions, identify your purpose, figure out your gifts and skills and how best to use them, make plans to make a difference, and start taking actual steps to pursue that purpose.

God planted a purpose in your heart long ago, and He is expecting you to find it and pursue it with Him. It is something that He chose specifically for you, something that will be meaningful and allow you to love and serve the people around you. It will be something that lights up your life, makes you feel fulfilled and positive, and, above all else, brings you ever closer to Him.

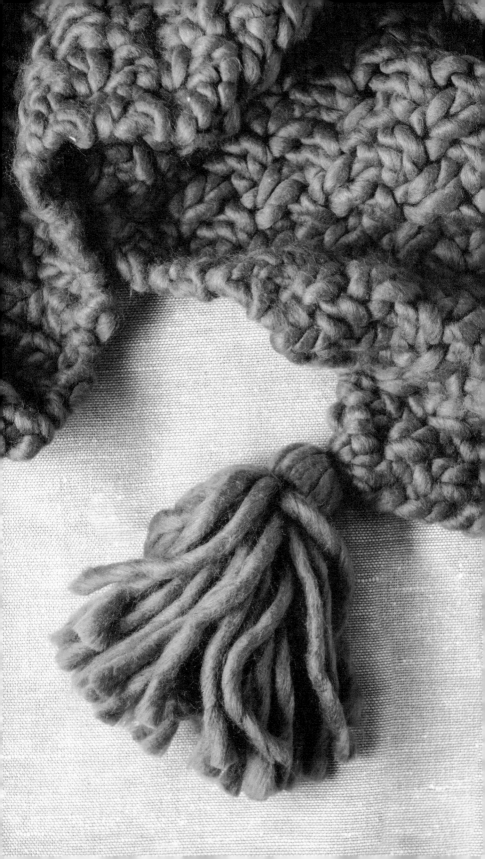

Discover Your Why

*Go, eat your food with gladness, and drink
your wine with a joyful heart, for God
has already approved what you do.*

ECCLESIASTES 9:7 NIV

P*urpose* is a big word. It can feel daunting to try to identify something so important. But *passion* isn't nearly as intimidating. After all, you can be passionate about a lot of things—little things like cute kittens or cold brew coffee and big things like your family or your career.

The good news is that God created you to be passionate about your purpose. He made you to fulfill your purpose joyfully. And each of us has our own unique purpose, suited to our talents and passions. A lot of us get down because we have a false idea of what our purpose *should* be, even if it's not something we're interested in. If the thought of living roughly fills you with dread, then God has not called you to be a missionary in a less-developed country. If you struggle around children, then God has likely not called you to teach. And you don't have to feel guilty about that. God has planted those purposes in other hearts. If you pursue someone else's purpose, who will take care of yours?

What are you passionate about? What things could you talk about for hours? What are you good at? Those things just might be arrows pointing you toward your purpose. What in the world breaks your heart? Whatever that is for you, it's time to dig into it a little further. That empathy is often God leading you toward the place you should be helping.

WEEK 1

Get to Know Yourself

The purpose in a man's heart is like deep water,
but a man of understanding will draw it out.

PROVERBS 20:5 ESV

God created you for a purpose. He blessed you with talents, skills, and passions that all allow you to pursue that purpose. God knows you, inside and out, and has already given you everything you need. But do you know yourself that well?

It's very difficult to find your purpose if you haven't taken the time to get to know yourself. To find your purpose, you need to know what lights you up inside, what you are really great at doing, and what you aren't so great at doing. You need to know what works well for you and what doesn't. Which things make you feel most alive and on fire, and which activities sap your strength and leave you exhausted? What do you want to be doing with your precious time and energy?

It's okay if you don't know what you want yet. But if you truly want to live your purpose, it's time to start figuring it out.

What do you most enjoy doing?

....

....

....

....

What are your biggest strengths? And weaknesses?

....

....

....

....

....

Describe how you are wired. What's in your
heart that makes you feel alive?

....

....

....

....

....

What Breaks Your Heart?

Even in laughter the heart may sorrow,
and the end of mirth may be grief.

PROVERBS 14:13 NKJV

As helpful as it is to know what lights you up inside, it's equally helpful to get honest about what breaks your heart. There are so many people who desperately need help in this world. But none of us can help everywhere we want to, and not every cause can be our purpose.

What is the issue that upsets you the most? When you watch the news, what's the story that makes you wonder who is helping or why the problem isn't solved? That empathy and desire to help comes straight from God. It's one of the ways He shows us where we need to be.

It can be all too easy to ignore that voice inside of us prompting us to do something and assume that someone else—someone better equipped—is handling it, but you won't ever find your purpose if you ignore the heartbreak. Embrace it and God will make sure you have everything you need to step up.

What breaks your heart in this world?

....

....

....

....

....

How do you think you can help?

....

....

....

....

....

....

....

....

Your Purpose Comes from God

Do not allow this world to mold you in its own image. Instead, be transformed from the inside out by renewing your mind. As a result, you will be able to discern what God wills and whatever God finds good, pleasing, and complete.

ROMANS 12:2 The Voice

You may have a lot of different passions in life, but not all of them are related to your purpose. So how do you know if something you're passionate about is your purpose or just another interest? Your purpose is something God has planted in your heart. If your might-be purpose contradicts God's Word or doesn't come from a place of love and helping others, then it probably isn't the real deal. There are a lot of things you can do with your life that our culture would applaud you for or tell you was fine, but that God wouldn't. Those things will not be your purpose.

> Do you truly feel like this potential purpose came from God? Why or why not?

....

....

....

How does this potential purpose align with God's Word?

9

Ask God

I cry out to God Most High, to God
who fulfills his purpose for me.

PSALM 57:2 ESV

Your purpose is never just yours. It will always be something that you share with God, and He wants to work alongside you to fulfill it. So it makes sense that the best way to discover your purpose is to ask God for His guidance. Pray and ask Him questions. Then embrace times of stillness so you can listen for His answers. Be on alert for those little nudges when God is pointing you in the right direction or leading you to someone who can help you. Talk to God about your purpose every chance you can. You may find the answers you need immediately, or it may take time, but eventually God will show you where He needs you.

> Pray to God and ask Him what your purpose is.
> Record any answers or nudges you get here.

....

....

....

....

What do you think God is trying to tell you?

....

....

....

....

....

....

....

....

....

....

....

....

....

....

Find Guidance in God's Word

Your word is a lamp for my feet, a light on my path.

PSALM 119:105 NIV

We can pray and pray and pray for answers, but we sometimes forget that God has given us a guidebook filled with His wisdom and answers. If, despite your prayers, you are still feeling stuck, crack open your Bible and start reading. You aren't the first and you certainly won't be the last person trying to find your purpose. The Bible is full of men and women who struggled to find and fulfill theirs too. Their stories might provide just the inspiration you need to find your own way.

> Keep track of any verses that really speak
> to you about your purpose here.

....

....

....

....

Which stories in particular feel applicable
to where you are on your journey?

....

....

....

....

....

....

....

....

....

....

....

....

....

Trust God

*Trust in the LORD with all your heart and
lean not on your own understanding.*

PROVERBS 3:5 NIV

It would sure be nice if finding your purpose was always straightforward and clear, but it likely won't be. It may be frustrating and confusing, and you may want to give up altogether sometimes. And even if it is easy for you, there will be times when you second-guess yourself and wonder just exactly what you've gotten yourself into, times when you feel utterly lost and fear you may have made a terrible mistake. This is normal.

We have to remember that our feelings are not trustworthy, but God is. Our feelings change from one moment to the next, but God doesn't. He is steadfast and true, always. When you feel lost, you can always trust God to guide you home.

> When have you felt frustrated and confused
> while pursuing your purpose?

....

....

....

How have your feelings led you astray?

....

....

....

....

How did you get back on track?

....

....

....

....

....

....

....

....

Unselfish

*Real religion, the kind that passes muster
before God the Father, is this: Reach out to the
homeless and loveless in their plight, and guard
against corruption from the godless world.*

JAMES 1:27 MSG

Close your eyes and think about the purpose you feel called
to. How would you describe it to someone else?

....

....

....

....

If what you wrote is all about you—your wants, your needs,
your reputation—then it likely is a dream and not a purpose. A
dream and a purpose are not the same thing, although they can
and often do overlap. Just like with passions, you will have a lot
of dreams in your lifetime. Some will be altruistic, and others
will be selfish—and that is absolutely okay! You should dream
for yourself. Just know that your purpose will be so much
bigger than just you. It will reflect God's love and be big and
bold and all about loving others.

What are some of the dreams you have for yourself?

....

....

....

....

....

Which ones are more about you? And which
ones are about loving others?

....

....

....

....

....

....

....

....

Help Others

If one part suffers, every part suffers with it; if one part is honored, every part rejoices with it.

1 CORINTHIANS 12:26 NIV

Your purpose will make a difference for the better in the world. You might not always be able to see that difference fully play out, but it isn't your purpose if it doesn't help others. Now that's not to say that your purpose has to involve helping others directly, face-to-face. You may be called to work in a lab searching for a cancer treatment. Perhaps you'll support an organization that helps foster children. Maybe you'll design a line of size-inclusive clothing that makes women feel great about themselves. Or you'll feel called to motherhood and pouring into your kids, one of whom may become an impactful leader in the community.

It's okay if your purpose isn't to open an orphanage or become a missionary. There are so many different ways to help. Let go of what you think you should do and focus on finding what you are uniquely suited to do.

What are some ways you are already helping
others through your passions?

....

....

....

....

....

....

....

....

How could you potentially take that to the next level?

....

....

....

....

From Love

"You must love the L<small>ORD</small> your God with all your heart, all your soul, and all your mind." This is the first and greatest commandment. A second is equally important: "Love your neighbor as yourself."

MATTHEW 22:37–39 <small>NLT</small>

We are all called to help and love each other. Jesus was really clear about that. There is not a single purpose that comes from God that doesn't involve loving Him and loving others—even others who don't look or act or talk or think just like us. As you work to discover what your purpose is, put that in the forefront of your mind. Meditate on the love and help you want to show your neighbors (even the tough-to-love ones!), and watch to see how God opens doors for you to do just that.

Are there people out there who you struggle to love?

....

....

....

....

How can you open your heart more fully to them?

Share Jesus

*Jesus, undeterred, went right ahead and gave his charge:
"God authorized and commanded me to commission
you: Go out and train everyone you meet, far and near, in
this way of life, marking them by baptism in the threefold
name: Father, Son, and Holy Spirit. Then instruct
them in the practice of all I have commanded you."*

MATTHEW 28:18–20 MSG

While every purpose is different, they all have one thing in common. We are all called to share the good news of God's great love for us and His sacrifice on the cross. Helping others isn't just about meeting their physical needs; it also involves meeting their spiritual needs. The absolute best way any of us can do that is by helping others get to know Jesus.

Sharing our faith is huge, but our actions matter just as much. If we talk about Jesus' love, but we don't speak and act with love in our daily lives, then our testimony won't make much of an impact. As Christians, part of our purpose is to live as much like Jesus as we can—to show love and compassion to everyone we meet, and to be a light to the world.

How have you been sharing Jesus' love with others lately?

How can you influence others who want to know
more about Jesus after spending time with you?

No Small Purpose

*Therefore, whether you eat or drink, or
whatever you do, do all to the glory of God.*

1 CORINTHIANS 10:31 NKJV

God doesn't see things the same way that we do. We may look at someone like Mother Teresa, who dedicated her life to helping the poor of Calcutta, and think that our purpose isn't as important as hers. But there is no winning or losing, no lesser than or greater than, when it comes to purpose. God needs each and every one of us to play our part. To Him, every purpose is important.

You can't see the big picture, so you can't see all the ways your actions contribute to His plan. But you can have faith that nothing is small or unimportant to God, and He has big plans for you and your purpose.

> When have you felt called to a specific purpose?

26

How are you pursuing it right now?

....

....

....

....

How do you feel about your purpose? Are your feelings holding you back or motivating you?

....

....

....

....

....

....

....

....

A Cheerful Heart

*Work hard and cheerfully at all you do,
just as though you were working for the
Lord and not merely for your masters.*

COLOSSIANS 3:23 TLB

Not every moment of pursuing your purpose will be fun and exciting and fulfilling. Oftentimes, we are called to put our heads down and slog through the drudgery that needs to be done. This is often where people get frustrated and give up. But this is also where God needs us most. Find ways to make this work fun, and keep reminding yourself that you are working for God's glory. If you ask, He will always share His joy.

What are the tasks you hate to do the most?

....

....

....

....

....

How can you make them more fun?

You Can't Ignore Your Purpose

*If anyone, then, knows the good they ought
to do and doesn't do it, it is sin for them.*

JAMES 4:17 NIV

Your purpose isn't optional. It's not something you can politely decline or reject for a different choice. God has called you, and He is waiting for you to find your path and get going. He chose you for this purpose. Really think about that. Out of the millions of other people in the world, God chose you. You were, quite literally, made for this.

Saying no or ignoring the call puts a wedge between you and God and interferes with your ability to develop a close relationship with Him. He didn't choose your purpose to make you miserable or uncomfortable. He chose to bless you through your purpose, to give you a hope and a future. God has so much in store for you that you can't see yet, and you can't get to it until you embrace who you were created to be. So what are you waiting for? It's time to get started!

Do you think you know your purpose, but feel
reluctant or uncomfortable to pursue it? Why?

....

....

....

....

What happened in the past when you answered God's call?

....

....

....

....

How can you trust God to bless you through this purpose?

....

....

....

....

Gifts

How Has God Prepared You for Your Purpose?

There are different kinds of spiritual gifts, but they all come from the same Spirit. There are different ways to serve the same Lord, and we can each do different things. Yet the same God works in all of us and helps us in everything we do.

1 CORINTHIANS 12:4–6 CEV

Your purpose is an integral part of you. It was planted in your heart when you were created, and God has equipped you with everything you need to fulfill it. You may not *feel* like you have everything you need, but it's all there.

God has blessed each of us with gifts and strengths, things that we do well naturally, like running or organizing or bookkeeping. But our strengths also include innate social skills, like the ability to calm a crowd, or the talent to get someone to open up and talk to us. They also include those indefinable qualities that can't be taught, such as the ability to invent new ways to do things, or to come up with the perfect business strategy.

Even more than that, God gives each of us the life experiences we need to grow those skills and mold our perspectives. Sure, you may share a lot of skills or strengths with others you know, but certainly not all of them. And no one else has ever lived the life you have. All of these things combined make you *the* person for *the* job, which is the purpose God has selected just for you.

Unique

*We look at this Son and see God's original purpose
in everything created. For everything, absolutely
everything, above and below, visible and invisible,
rank after rank after rank of angels—everything
got started in him and finds its purpose in him.*

COLOSSIANS 1:16 MSG

God didn't make you *you* by accident. He didn't just throw in a few personality traits at random and call you good. No, God created you with care specifically for your unique purpose. He selected each of your talents, strengths, weaknesses, skills, passions, interests, and idiosyncrasies with care and intention. He carefully chose your family, neighbors, teachers, mentors, bosses, and coworkers to make sure you had the opportunities to learn the lessons you needed to grow. He watched and guided you as you moved through life—falling in love, getting your heart broken, making and losing friendships, learning about the world, and discovering more about yourself. And He was there with arms wide open when you dedicated your life to Him.

None of that happened by accident, chance, or coincidence. You and your unique purpose are a carefully orchestrated part of God's plans.

When have you ever felt unqualified or unprepared for what God has called you to do?

....

....

....

....

....

....

Where do you feel you need to grow to continue to pursue your purpose? What plan can you make for that?

....

....

....

....

....

....

It Is Good

Everything good comes from God.
Every perfect gift is from him.

JAMES 1:17 ERV

If God gave you a gift, it is a good thing. Depending on the culture and family you grew up in, though, you might not have always believed that. Different families and cultures value different talents and skills and look down on others. But God doesn't have the same prejudices. Your family might have looked down on a naturally commanding nature and called you bossy, but God gave you leadership skills for a reason. Your community might have preferred inside-the-box thinking, which always made you feel like an outcast, but God needs your creativity to make you a resourceful problem solver.

God's ways are not the world's ways. They are far, far better. We, as people, are flawed, and our prejudices and biases are flawed too. Don't miss out on your purpose because you let the world's ways trump God's ways.

> Are there any talents, skills, or gifts that you haven't been using because others told you that you shouldn't?

....

....

....

....

....

....

> Have you ever assumed any of your strengths
> were actually weaknesses? Which ones?

....

....

....

....

....

....

....

....

Don't Hide Your Talents

"Let your light so shine before men, that they may see your good works and glorify your Father in heaven."

MATTHEW 5:16 NKJV

If you gave a dear friend something she desperately needed to do her job and she refused to use it, would you be frustrated? God has given you *everything* you need to pursue your purpose. Are you using it all?

Are there things you're great at, but you feel like they don't matter? Skills you assume aren't special enough? Experiences that you always downplay? Maybe you were teased for your gifts in the past or made to feel like your skills were less than, so you just stopped using them. Or maybe others around you had the same skills, so you always let them step forward instead.

You've dulled your light. But God has more in mind for you. You were made to shine brightly, to lead others to God like a beacon in the darkness. You need to use your gifts—all of them—if you hope to achieve your purpose.

Do you feel like you shine? Or have you
been hiding your light? Why?

....

....

....

Which gifts has God given you that you haven't been using?

....

....

....

....

How could you put those underutilized gifts to good use?

....

....

....

....

WEEK 17

Serve

As each has received a gift, use it to serve one
another, as good stewards of God's varied grace.

1 PETER 4:10 ESV

While it's important to use your gifts in all areas of your life, it's especially important to use the gifts God has given you to serve others. God does not give us selfish purposes. We were created to care for one another, and there are so many ways to serve. Your gift of organization can help a nonprofit get volunteers coordinated. Your gift of foresight can help the PTA plan ahead better to serve teachers. Your gift of connection can help comfort and encourage kids at the youth center.

Think about those heartbreaking injustices and situations you wrote down earlier. How can your gifts and strengths allow you to help?

> Brainstorm a list of organizations with missions that match up with the things that break your heart in this world.

....

....

....

....

How can your talents and gifts help at these organizations? Think outside of the box.

....

....

....

....

....

....

....

Does one of the organizations jump out? What one step can you start with to pitch them on your ideas?

....

....

....

....

....

....

Master Your Skills

*"If you have any skills, you should use them
to help make what I have commanded."*

EXODUS 35:10 CEV

God gifted you the skills and talents, but it's up to you to practice them, grow them, master them, and, ultimately, use them. He will give you the opportunities, make sure the right people cross your tracks, and inspire you—but it is up to you, and *only* you, to grab a hold of those chances and use them. If you aren't willing to do that work to prepare your gifts, what will you do when He calls you to use them?

God doesn't *make* anyone pursue a purpose. We have free will. But God certainly does want us to *choose* to pursue our purpose because we love and trust Him and are obedient to His calling. Mastering your skills and talents is one way of saying, "Yes, God! I'm ready for the purpose You chose for me."

> Which of your gifts needs to be practiced and improved?

....

....

....

....

....

....

....

....

....

How can you go about obediently sharpening those skills?

....

....

....

....

....

....

....

....

The Holy Spirit Equips

"I have filled him with the Spirit of God, with ability and intelligence, with knowledge and all craftsmanship."

EXODUS 31:3 ESV

One of the biggest things that hold people back from pursuing their purpose is the nagging feeling that they don't have what it takes. They think they lack the experience or education or talent to make a real difference. They believe that they need to be more capable, smarter, or *better* to even get started.

How silly is that when you really think about it? It doesn't matter if *you* don't have what it takes because *God* has it in abundance. When you show up where He has called you, ready to get to work, God will equip you. The Holy Spirit never leaves you and will be right there to give you everything you need if you just commit to getting started.

What are a few things you've always wanted
to do but not felt equipped for?

How can you challenge yourself to show up and
trust God to give you what you need?

Good Deeds

*For we are His workmanship—created in
Messiah Yeshua for good deeds, which God
prepared beforehand so we might walk in them.*

EPHESIANS 2:10 TLV

Pursuing your purpose doesn't mean wandering around aimlessly trying to figure out what to do. Before you were born, God thought through what He was calling you to and prepared good works for you to do. Not just deeds or works, but *good* deeds.

Isn't that a relief? You don't have to figure it all out yourself because God has already drawn the map. And He's already called it good. All you have to do is show up in faith and start taking steps. God will make your path straight and lead you to where you need to be. Keep trusting Him, step after step, and you will find your way.

> Think back on your lifelong pursuit of your purpose.
> What good deeds and works have you already done?

....

....

....

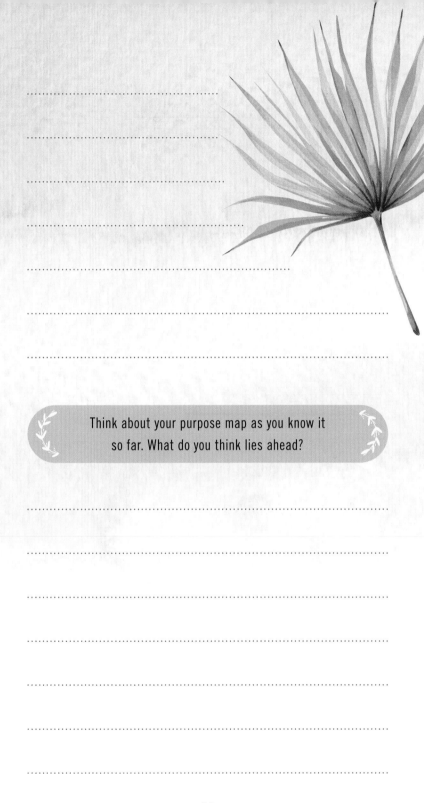

....

....

....

....

....

....

....

Think about your purpose map as you know it
so far. What do you think lies ahead?

....

....

....

....

....

....

A Lifelong Pursuit

*And I am certain that God, who began
the good work within you, will continue
his work until it is finally finished on
the day when Christ Jesus returns.*

PHILIPPIANS 1:6 NLT

It's always nice to see the results of our hard work, to appreciate the final result of all of those late nights, early mornings, and sacrifices. But that isn't always possible when it comes to purpose. If God has called you to work on global, systemic issues like poverty, oppression, or protecting the rights of children, well, it's unlikely that you will see your purpose completely fulfilled in your lifetime.

But just because you won't live to see the end of poverty or oppression doesn't mean that your work isn't making a real difference. Some of us see a lot of progress, but others barely see any movement. However, to God, it's not how successful you are; it's how hard you work, how obedient you are to what He has called you to do. In the end, He will be victorious, fulfilling every purpose and righting every wrong.

Has God called you to something where you think you'll see a lot of success? What would that look like to you?

....

....

....

....

....

....

How do you handle it when successes are few and far between?

....

....

....

....

....

Avoid the Comparison Trap

*In his grace, God has given us different
gifts for doing certain things well.*

ROMANS 12:6 NLT

That word *grace* matters so much in this verse. It doesn't mean forgiveness here; it means kindness or benevolence. Out of His *kindness*, God chose to give each of us different gifts. Think about what it would be like if we were all exactly the same. Talk about causing comparison! But since we are each unique, God looks at what we have done with what He has given us—not what He gave to anyone else.

Envy and comparison can stop your purpose pursuit right in its tracks. They will trap you and keep you stuck. But you can combat them by finding the root cause. Push past the bad feelings. What does that envy reveal about the state of your heart? If you envy a friend's people skills, you may be longing for more connection. If you envy a coworker's efficiency, you may be longing to find more time to fulfill your purpose. If you envy another mom's leadership, you may be longing for the confidence to step up and make a difference.

Who do you compare yourself to often?

What do those comparisons tell you about your own longings?

We Are All Unique

*Isn't it obvious that a potter has a perfect right
to shape one lump of clay into a vase for holding
flowers and another into a pot for cooking beans?*

ROMANS 9:21 MSG

God made each of us different to serve different purposes.
You don't have to be just like that girl on social media with
100,000 followers or the parents on the PTA or even your best
friends.

Your life won't look like their lives because your purpose
is different than theirs. That can be tough to accept, especially
when it seems like everyone else's lives are more exciting or
important or fun than yours. But flashy excitement doesn't
mean anything in God's eyes. What He has called you to do may
not be fancy, but that doesn't mean it isn't vitally important.
The vase holding flowers may seem more glamorous, but most
people *need* the pot to cook beans more!

What kind of vessel do you think God made you to be? Why?

....

....

....

....

....

....

....

....

Is there another type of container you wish you were? Why?

....

....

....

....

....

....

....

Each Gift Matters

The Spirit has given each of us a special way of serving others. Some of us can speak with wisdom, while others can speak with knowledge, but these gifts come from the same Spirit. To others the Spirit has given great faith or the power to heal the sick or the power to work mighty miracles. Some of us are prophets, and some of us recognize when God's Spirit is present. Others can speak different kinds of languages, and still others can tell what these languages mean. But it is the Spirit who does all this and decides which gifts to give to each of us.

1 CORINTHIANS 12:7–11 CEV

Each of us has been given different gifts and talents, but they all come from the same Holy Spirit, and they all matter. Your gifts and someone else's gifts won't be the same, but they might complement each other. It's the same with purpose. Often your purpose and their purpose, while different, can come together to create amazing results neither of you could have ever dreamed of. But that doesn't surprise God one bit.

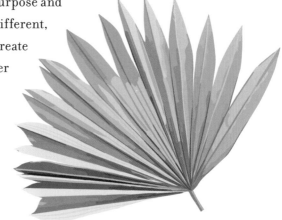

When has your purpose led you to work with someone whose gifts amplified your own and helped you achieve big things?

....

....

....

....

....

....

Is there someone in your life who is working toward their purpose and could use a helping hand?

....

....

....

....

....

....

In Community

*He joins and holds together the whole body
with its ligaments providing the support
needed so each part works to its proper
design to form a healthy, growing, and
mature body that builds itself up in love.*

EPHESIANS 4:16 The Voice

We were created to live in community, to use our complementary gifts to love and serve others. None of us was ever meant to go through life alone. None of us is equipped with every gift needed to fulfill our purposes alone. It's only by working together, as the body of Christ, that we can do the big things God asks us to do. When we work together for His glory in our callings, we can accomplish truly miraculous things.

Do you work well with others? Why or why not?

What is going unfulfilled because you can't
tackle it alone? Who can you ask for help?

God Chose YOU

*You are a chosen people, a royal priesthood,
a holy nation, God's special possession, that
you may declare the praises of him who called
you out of darkness into his wonderful light.*

1 PETER 2:9 NIV

Out of the billions of people walking the earth right now,
God chose *you* for your purpose. God sees you, knows your
heart, and gave you everything you need to do good work for
Him and His kingdom. You are God's special possession, which
He loves and favors. How amazing does that make you feel?

The work you do while pursuing your purpose, the people
you meet, and the lives you change are all to lead people to
Him. The purpose you've been called to is important, but God
can use the impact you make along the way to make an even
bigger difference, bringing more glory to Him.

> How does it feel to know that you have
> been chosen specifically by God?

....

....

....

In what ways have you made a difference
that you weren't expecting?

Vision

How God Wants You to Help

It's in Christ that we find out who we are and what we are living for. Long before we first heard of Christ and got our hopes up, he had his eye on us, had designs on us for glorious living, part of the overall purpose he is working out in everything and everyone.

EPHESIANS 1:11–12 MSG

Once you have a firm idea of your purpose, it's time to figure out exactly how you want to pursue it. You've cataloged your skills, gifts, and talents, so you're ready to plan. But this isn't something you really can or should do on your own. This is something you should do *with* God. His ways are the best ways. He sees the whole tapestry, while you may only see a few threads.

You can brainstorm for days, attend seminars, do research, speak to experts, and read every self-help book on the market, but none of that will help if you haven't brought God into the process. So how do you do that? It's simple. 1) Pray, 2) Listen for God's response, 3) Execute, and 4) Repeat.

Now that's not to say you shouldn't give it your all. You absolutely should! Get creative, think on your feet, and search for solutions—but also pray while you do. Keep praying, keep listening to God, and keep saying yes to whatever He asks you to do, and your plans will turn into a purpose fulfilled for His glory.

Who Are You Serving?

So be very careful how you live, not being
like those with no understanding, but live
honorably with true wisdom, for we are living
in evil times. Take full advantage of every
day as you spend your life for his purposes.

EPHESIANS 5:15–16 TPT

Our world values very different things than what God values, and those things can be very distracting. Notoriety and success, money and security, and keeping up with the Joneses can all keep us from prioritizing our pursuit of purpose. This is as true now as it was in Jesus' day, and people are just as distracted as they ever were. In fact, we have so many more distractions now—social media, television, twenty-four-hour news. It is all too easy to start living for what our culture values, especially when what God asks of us isn't as cool or popular. But pursuing your purpose means focusing on what God values and what God expects of you, not what your neighbors value and expect of you.

What is your biggest distraction to getting God's work done?

....

....

....

....

....

....

How can you best counter that distraction so
you don't let it knock you offtrack?

....

....

....

....

....

Be Bold

*"Take the thousand and give it to the one
who risked the most. And get rid of this
'play-it-safe' who won't go out on a limb.
Throw him out into utter darkness."*

MATTHEW 25:28–30 MSG

These verses come from the parable of the talents, a story Jesus told about a rich man who went on a journey and left some of his money to be invested by three servants. The first two servants invested the money and increased it while the rich man was away, but the last servant buried the money he'd been given in the ground. Technically, no money was lost, but no money was gained either.

God is looking at how you handle your purpose, the responsibility He's entrusted to you here on earth, in the same way the rich man looked at how his servants handled his money. God fully expects a return on His investment. He doesn't want anyone to play it safe. He wants us to be bold, to take risks to achieve our purpose and bring glory to Him and His kingdom.

How are you working to bring God a return on His investment?

....

....

....

....

....

What do you think the parable means for anyone
who plays it safe with their purpose?

....

....

....

....

....

....

....

....

Make Plans with God

In their hearts humans plan their course,
but the LORD establishes their steps.

PROVERBS 16:9 NIV

It is wise to make plans before acting—to gather information, learn as much as you can, and come up with scenarios that should lead to success. Going in blind rarely gets you as far as planning does. That said, our plans don't hold a candle to God's plans. God is the original long-term planner. His plans are intricate, beautiful, and dramatic, and they cover millions of years. So doesn't it make sense to invite God into your planning? Pray over every plan you make, and invite God to establish your steps so that they are in line with His plans.

> How developed are the plans you have for pursuing your purpose? How flexible are they if something goes wrong?

Pray over those plans. Listen for God's feedback. How would you revise those plans with God's input?

Ask for Help

*Plans fail for lack of counsel, but with
many advisers they succeed.*

PROVERBS 15:22 NIV

No one is going to give you a badge for going it alone. So many people want to do everything themselves, to make it without any help, because they think it makes them tough or strong or successful in a way that no one can criticize. But God tells us that this is not the way to succeed. God wants us to help each other. He wants you to help others in need, *and* He wants you to receive help when you need it.

Refusing wise counsel and help is letting pride take over, and as the Bible tells us in Proverbs 16:18, "Pride goes before destruction" (NIV). That is one of the most-quoted verses for a good reason. Instead of giving in to pride, ask for help. Have your business-savvy friend look over your business plan, ask your pastor to pray for your mission work, or have your family give you feedback on your new product design. Whatever your purpose is, lean on your community for support, encouragement, advice, and information.

Who in your life would make an excellent adviser
when it comes to your pursuit of purpose?

....

....

....

....

....

Other than advice, what else can you lean on
your community for to support you in this?

....

....

....

....

....

....

Be Flexible

*Many are the plans in a person's heart, but
it is the Lord's purpose that prevails.*

PROVERBS 19:21 NIV

When you say yes to pursuing your purpose, you are saying yes to all the setbacks and surprises and detours that come along with that. Yes, some of them will be tough. But some of them will be wonderful, miraculous, pinch-me-is-this-really-happening sort of things! When you put your trust in God to direct your steps, anything can happen because nothing is impossible for Him.

So when you hit a snag or need to change course, try to be flexible and open to what may come. Let God lead the way, and do your best to keep up. Trust that your holy Father has something in store for you that is so much better than anything you could dream up for yourself.

> When has everything gone wrong, but it
> led you to something amazing?

....

....

....

....

....

....

....

....

Do you consider yourself flexible? Or do setbacks
and detours make you feel queasy? Why is that?

....

....

....

....

....

....

....

Follow Him

Then he said to the crowd, "If any of you wants to be my follower, you must give up your own way, take up your cross daily, and follow me."

LUKE 9:23 NLT

Jesus is very clear in this week's verse. To follow Him, we must give up our own ways. If you like to be in full control at all times, this one is a doozy! Even if you don't mind going with the flow, this one can still be a challenge. Why? Because God's ways are not our ways. Our society is not the same as the perfect kingdom He is building for us. Our expectations and assumptions just don't always align.

God knows that. He knows what a struggle this can be for us. But Jesus tells His listeners to follow Him because it is important for us to remember that God's ways are greater than our ways—every time and in every instance. Your purpose comes from God, and it needs to be pursued in God's way. So keep praying and keep following Him.

When have you felt like your way of doing
things was clashing with God's ways?

....

....

....

....

....

....

....

What happened when you tried things His way?

....

....

....

....

....

Plans for Good

*"For I know the plans I have for you," declares
the Lᴏʀᴅ, "plans to prosper you and not to harm
you, plans to give you hope and a future."*

JEREMIAH 29:11 (ɴɪᴠ)

This week's verse says it all. God has plans for you. He has plans for your purpose. And they are wonderful plans. The uncertainties in life can get to all of us sometimes. Earth is not an easy place to live with political unrest, environmental disasters, inflation, and wars. The news alone is enough to keep you up at night. Add to all that the everyday stresses of your job, keeping your family fed, and keeping your house clean(ish), and it's no wonder so many of us are stressed out, burnt out, and anxious.

But how wonderful is this promise from God? He doesn't promise His plans will be easy or simple or that you will always be happy, but He does promise that He has plans to prosper you and to give you hope and a future.

What makes you anxious most often? What is it about that situation that triggers your worries and stress?

....

....

....

....

....

....

....

....

Have you prayed about that anxiety
specifically? Why or why not?

....

....

....

....

....

....

....

God's Way

*The Lord Almighty has sworn, "Surely,
as I have planned, so it will be, and as
I have purposed, so it will happen."*

ISAIAH 14:24 NIV

We might sometimes feel unsure of or less than confident in our purpose pursuits, but God never does. He never doubts or gives up on us. God will make sure that what He has said will happen happens. He is so confident about it that He *swears* it.

Here's the thing. God doesn't need us. He doesn't need you to fulfill your purpose for His plans to work out. He has given each of us a purpose as a gift. This is our chance to show God that we can be trusted to obey and work for Him. Your purpose is an opportunity to live out God's Word. Your purpose will draw you closer to God; it will help refine your heart and shift your priorities to more closely align with God's priorities. It will do good in the world, but it will also do so much good in you.

In what ways do you think your purpose is a gift?

How has pursuing your purpose changed
your relationship with God?

Made for This

*"Before I shaped you in the womb, I knew
all about you. Before you saw the light
of day, I had holy plans for you."*

JEREMIAH 1:5 MSG

Nothing about you was an accident. Everything about you was planned and purposeful. There has not been a moment of your existence when you were not known and loved by God. You were made for a purpose. You were put on this earth to fulfill God's holy plans, not to have fun or become successful or even to become a spouse or a parent (though none of those things are bad!). You are here to fulfill the holy plans God designed before you were even born.

> How do you feel when you *really* think about the fact that God knew and had plans for you before you were born?

....

....

....

....

How does knowing you were made for your purpose
change how you feel about your work?

Legacy

*The plans of the LORD stand firm forever, the
purposes of his heart through all generations.*

PSALM 33:11 NIV

You may not accomplish everything you work toward in this lifetime. Some of God's holy plans require generations' worth of time. Those who come after you will be called to build upon the work that you have done, and others will build on their work until the day that work is complete. What you do here and now affects all of the people who come after you—the children whose lives you impact, and their children, grandchildren, and great-grandchildren. The things that you *fail* to do also affect the generations to come.

Every time you say yes to God, you are building up that foundation for future generations. But every time you ignore your calling, you are putting future generations behind. Your work leaves behind a legacy. It's up to you to decide whether it will be a bad one or a good one.

> Does your purpose stop with you, or is it tied to something bigger? Does your purpose pass on to others?

....

....

....

....

....

....

....

What kind of legacy do you think you will
leave behind through your purpose?

....

....

....

....

....

Perfect Timing

*To everything there is a season, a time
for every purpose under heaven.*

ECCLESIASTES 3:1 NKJV

Your purpose, like everything else in life, will go through seasons. Sometimes you are in a season of work and productivity, and sometimes you are in a season of rest. Sometimes you are in a season of action, and sometimes you are in a season of planning. Every season will help you grow and accomplish all you need to in order to bring your personal purpose to fruition.

God does not expect instant success. In fact, He has always planned for things to take time—His divine time—to get to that point. In a garden, you can't see growth in the winter or harvest in the spring. In the same way, there are certain things regarding your purpose that can only happen in specific seasons. Take advantage of each season that comes along to do the work that comes with it.

Which season do you think your purpose is in right now?

....

....

....

....

What can you accomplish only in this particular
season? How can you get those things done?

....

....

....

....

....

....

....

Work Together

*The one who plants and the one who waters
have one purpose, and they will each be
rewarded according to their own labor.*

1 CORINTHIANS 3:8 NIV

Your purpose is only part of God's greater plan. You may not be able to see it now, but your purpose and others' purposes will someday fit together to produce God-sized results.

Your purpose will always be your purpose, but it is important to remember that it's only one piece of the puzzle. God will put people around you with the other pieces He needs to finish His puzzle. He wants you to work with them, to be part of His larger community, His larger kingdom.

This can be tough if you would rather work solo or if you find it challenging to work with others. Working with other people requires trust. Remember that even if it's scary to trust others, you can always trust God, so the people He leads you to are worth trusting too.

Why is it sometimes frustrating trying
to work with other people?

....

....

....

....

....

....

....

How might you ensure your specific purpose doesn't
get lost in the bigger goals of a group of people?

....

....

....

....

....

....

All In

*Listen, there's nothing wrong with zeal
when you're zealous for God's good purpose.
And what's more, you don't have to wait
for me to be with you to seek the good.*

GALATIANS 4:18 THE VOICE

Your purpose should be something that lights you up inside, something you are excited about and can't wait to get started on each day. It should be something that fills you with passion. If you aren't feeling that way right now, think about what is holding you back. Is it how you feel about your work, or is it how you think others will respond to your ardent pursuit? How society will view your plans?

Don't let anyone convince you to chill out about your purpose or be more cautious. Don't let anyone convince you that your purpose is wrong because it doesn't mesh with what's cool or trendy. God doesn't want you to be cautious or hold back. He wants you to go all in with Him, because His opinion is the only one that matters.

How do you feel about your purpose?

....

....

....

....

....

....

How can you plan to overcome any negative
opinions about your purpose?

....

....

....

....

....

....

Action

Fulfill Your Purpose

Then I heard the voice of the Lord saying, "Whom shall I send?
And who will go for us?" And I said, "Here am I. Send me!"

ISAIAH 6:8 NIV

Thinking, planning, and preparing are all well and good, but none of those things will actually fulfill your purpose. To do that you have to act. God doesn't instruct us to overthink everything to death. He instructs us to obey. To hear His call, accept His instructions, and get to work.

In the parable of the two sons (Matthew 21:28–32), a father told each of his two sons to go work in his vineyard that day. The first son at first refused to work, but then he later changed his mind and went and did what his father asked of him. The second son promised to go, but then he never did the work he committed to doing. Jesus asked the crowd, "Which of the two did what his father wanted?" The answer, of course, was the first son. The second son said all the right things, but he never acted. Thinking about your purpose and making plans don't count. When God calls us, He expects action.

You will always be able to find a good excuse not to act. After all, life is busy and complicated, and there will always be a lot of demands on your time. It is up to you to choose: to keep up with the demands and expectations of society or to obediently say yes to God. Even if, like the first son, you have said no to your purpose time and again, it is not too late to change your mind and go do what your Father has asked of you.

Live Your Purpose

He has saved us and called us to a holy life—
not because of anything we have done but
because of his own purpose and grace.

2 TIMOTHY 1:9 NIV

God called *you* to a holy, purposeful life with Him to fulfill His greater plan and purpose. There's nothing you could have done or not done to earn such a distinction. It was given to you because of His grace and love. That is huge!

God is trusting *you* to do something for Him, to further His plans, to bring glory to His kingdom. Not because He needs the help, but because He wants to do it with you. Can you think of a bigger honor? Even if you feel unprepared or scared or uncertain, it's time to accept that trust and step into the purpose that He has prepared for you alone. God has put His faith in you, so it's time to put your faith in Him. Trust that He knows exactly what He's doing and answer His call.

> When you think about God trusting you with a holy purpose, how does it make you feel?

....

....

....

....

> What most inspires you to get going and act,
> even if you feel scared or unsure?

....

....

....

....

....

....

Chase Joy

So I commend the enjoyment of life, because
there is nothing better for a person under the
sun than to eat and drink and be glad. Then joy
will accompany them in their toil all the days
of the life God has given them under the sun.

ECCLESIASTES 8:15 NIV

Your purpose should not feel like a heavy burden or a drag. God created this purpose for you and you for this purpose. It's a part of you, something important and fulfilling, just like your relationship with God.

If what you think is your purpose fills you with dread and feels like a chore, then that isn't really your purpose. Your purpose, although it may be difficult or discouraging at times, should be joyful, meaningful work. Sometimes we can let our anxieties and stress overwhelm the joy. When that happens, it's time to pray and ask God to replace your worries with His peace so you can find that joy again.

What is holding you back from joy in your pursuit of your purpose? Why is it a stumbling block?

....

....

....

....

....

....

What brings you true joy in your purposeful work?

....

....

....

....

....

....

Keep Talking to God

"I have not ever acted, and will not in the future act, on My own. I listen to the directions of the One who sent Me and act on these divine instructions. For this reason, My judgment is always fair and never self-serving. I'm committed to pursuing God's agenda and not My own."

JOHN 5:30 THE VOICE

There will always be times when things don't go according to plan. No matter how long you've spent on the plans or how airtight they seem, you can't control everything. Pursuing your purpose in the face of obstacles and detours will require you to be flexible, creative, and, most importantly, a prayer warrior. When it's time to change your plans, the best counsel you can receive is God's.

Pray about your purpose every day. Keep God looped in about what you are learning, get His advice for overcoming the obstacles you encounter, and celebrate your success with Him. Keep talking to God and keep listening. He won't ever steer you wrong.

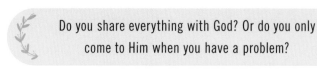

Do you share everything with God? Or do you only come to Him when you have a problem?

....

....

....

....

....

How many times a week do you ask for God's wisdom
and instructions? Do you think that's enough?

....

....

....

....

....

....

....

....

....

Justice, Mercy, Humility

He has shown you, O mortal, what is good. And what does the Lord require of you? To act justly and to love mercy and to walk humbly with your God.

MICAH 6:8 NIV

It is important to keep the ultimate goal of your purpose and who you serve in mind as you pursue your goals. God's purpose for you will never require you to stray from the path He has called good. Our society, on the other hand, is more than happy to make you question His plans for you. The world can be a very distracting place, and it is easier than you might think to drift off course.

Luckily, God has given us clear instructions to keep us on track. We are to act justly, love mercy, and walk humbly with Him. As long as you prioritize those things, the distractions of this world won't stand a chance.

How do God's dictums for justice, mercy, and humility fit within your purpose?

Do you feel like you are acting justly, loving mercy, and walking humbly with God right now? Why or why not?

You Don't Need an Audience

"When you do something for someone else, don't call attention to yourself. You've seen them in action, I'm sure—'playactors' I call them—treating prayer meeting and street corner alike as a stage, acting compassionate as long as someone is watching, playing to the crowds. They get applause, true, but that's all they get. When you help someone out, don't think about how it looks. Just do it—quietly and unobtrusively. That is the way your God, who conceived you in love, working behind the scenes, helps you out."

MATTHEW 6:2–4 MSG

God doesn't ask you to help and serve one another so that you can bolster your reputation or receive a round of applause. He wants you to show mercy to others the same way He shows mercy to you, quietly and without drawing attention to why you needed the help. He wants you to help because you genuinely love and care for others, just like He genuinely loves and cares for you—and because caring for others for their sakes, not your own, brings you closer to Him.

> How do you choose when and whom to help?

....

....

....

....

....

....

....

....

What most inspires you to serve others?

....

....

....

....

....

....

....

Walk the Walk

*"Not everyone who calls me their Lord will
get into the kingdom of heaven. Only the ones
who obey my Father in heaven will get in."*

MATTHEW 7:21 CEV

There are a lot of people who claim to love God and claim to be pursuing the purpose that He has called them to, but who, in the secret corners of their hearts, haven't obeyed His calling for their lives. While they may fool everyone around them, they never fool God. Their lives never produce the spiritual fruit that a true relationship with God produces.

For God, it's not enough to talk the talk. You have to walk the walk. Your life has to bear spiritual fruit. If you truly love God, saying yes to His calling is a pleasure, a privilege. When He rules your heart, you want to do His work and pursue His purpose for your life. If you are struggling to get past thinking about your purpose and into taking action, ask yourself what is holding you back.

> Who do you know talked the talk but never acted on it?

....

....

....

....

....

How are you walking the walk right now?

....

....

....

....

....

Nothing Is Impossible with God

*I can do all things through Christ
who strengthens me.*

PHILIPPIANS 4:13 NKJV

Doing the work to pursue your purpose won't always be easy. Some days your work will be sunshine and victory laps, and other times it will be all uphill, walking through the darkness, going on faith. But no matter how impossible it seems, you are never alone. God will always be right there beside you.

Life will inevitably throw you curveballs, send you on winding detours, and, from time to time, stop you right in your tracks with no foreseeable way forward at all. When the obstacles you face are insurmountable for you, they won't be insurmountable for God. God can make a way where there has never been one before. He can open doors that have long been locked tight. He can topple mountains, part seas, and raze whole cities for His purposes. There is nothing that is impossible when you are working with Him.

When have you ever faced something impossible
only to have God come through for you?

....

....

....

....

....

What is the most miraculous thing from God you
have personally witnessed or experienced?

....

....

....

....

....

....

Go Bigger

God can do anything, you know—far more
than you could ever imagine or guess or
request in your wildest dreams! He does it not
by pushing us around but by working within
us, his Spirit deeply and gently within us.

EPHESIANS 3:20 MSG

When you let God's Spirit in, when you let Him guide you and work within you, you will be able to go farther, dream bigger, and accomplish so much more than you ever could by yourself. Don't be afraid to keep pushing past what seems possible, past what feels doable. When you reach one bar, set another even higher. Go bigger in faith, trusting that God can and will get you there. When you let Him work within you, He will give you everything you need and put you where you need to be to go past anything you could envision in your wildest dreams.

> What is the biggest goal that you've set for yourself?
> What would success look like to you?

....

....

....

....

....

....

Now amplify that by ten. What does that
look like? By twenty? By thirty?

....

....

....

....

....

....

....

God Will Never Leave You

The Lord will fulfill his purpose for me;
your steadfast love, O Lord, endures forever.
Do not forsake the work of your hands.

PSALM 138:8 ESV

When you answer His call, you can trust that God will never abandon you, never forsake you, never leave you to go it alone. He will always be there for you, working with you and for you, and His purpose for you will endure as well. You may not always hear Him speaking directly to you or feel Him close by, but that doesn't mean He isn't there. Keep talking to Him and working for Him. Rest in the promise that He will always be there.

> When do you feel closer to God and seem to hear Him more clearly and easily?

When have you felt farther away from God?
What caused that to change?

Work for His Glory

*"I have raised you up for this very purpose,
that I might show you my power and that my
name might be proclaimed in all the earth."*

EXODUS 9:16 NIV

Your purpose may bring you fame, recognition, and success. Or it might not. God has called some of us to the spotlight and some of us to obscurity. But He has called all of us to glorify Him. None of us should be working for our own glory, but for His.

If you are in the spotlight, it's doubly important that your actions and words show your commitment to God's work. Your life should reflect the love He has shown you, which will lead others to Him. If you are working in less conspicuous ways, don't think that your work matters any less. Even if you aren't seen by millions, you are seen. You never know who is watching and who might be inspired by all you are doing.

Has your work brought you into the spotlight?
Or are you working outside of it?

....

....

....

....

....

If you are in the spotlight, how are you
reflecting that light back to God?

....

....

....

....

....

....

Keep Going

Hold firmly to the word of life; then, on the day of
Christ's return, I will be proud that I did not run the
race in vain and that my work was not useless.

PHILIPPIANS 2:16 NLT

The road to fulfilling your purpose will not be a straight, easy path. There will be uphills and downhills, potholes and curves, rocky sections as well as smooth ones. At times, you will feel like you can run forever, and other times each step will feel like it takes everything you have. Some days, it will feel far easier to give up than to take even one more step. But don't lose heart; keep going.

Turn to God's Word for strength and encouragement, pray for stamina and endurance, run alongside a buddy to keep you accountable. But don't give up. This race is worth it—worth the long nights and hard work, worth the blood, sweat, and tears, worth the pain. Let the finish line beckon you forward to eternal life with Him.

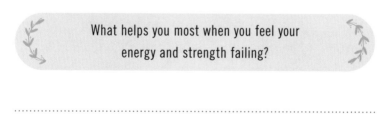

What helps you most when you feel your
energy and strength failing?

....

....

....

....

....

List out the verses here that encourage you
to keep going when you get tired.

....

....

....

....

....

....

....

....

Your Purpose Is His

*For from him and through him and for him are
all things. To him be the glory forever! Amen.*

ROMANS 11:36 NIV

Working diligently to fulfill your purpose will never be
a waste of your time. Regardless of how anyone else
may see it, your calling is not a vanity project or a
hobby or meaningless. Sometimes those around
us won't understand what God has called us to
do. Remember Noah? Everyone thought he
was insane for building an ark, but he knew
that God's calling trumped earthly opinions
every time.

You probably haven't been called to
build an ark in your backyard, but that
doesn't mean that some of your purpose
won't look strange to others. Hold tight to
your calling and have faith that God will
make it all make sense in time. Your purpose
is His purpose, and He always has His reasons
for doing the things He does. As you watch His
plans build, in time you will be able to see how
your calling contributed to His glory.

Has any part of your purpose really surprised you? Why?

....

....

....

....

....

....

Have your friends or family had trouble understanding your purpose or your dedication to your calling? How so?

....

....

....

....

....

....

Eternal Purpose

The world and its desires pass away, but
whoever does the will of God lives forever.

1 JOHN 2:17 NIV

Our lives on earth are so short. Even if you live to be 120 years old, that is but a blip when compared to the eternal life we are promised with Jesus. The things here that seem so important to you now—your social circle, your career, making sure your kids get into a good college—all of it will fade away once you are standing with Jesus. But your purpose will not. God has called you to this thing for a reason, and His work, His reasons are eternal. Of course, you can't say for certain what your time in heaven will look like, but it is likely that your purpose may figure into that. God has promised to finish the good works He began in your heart, and when the time comes, it will be a truly glorious day.

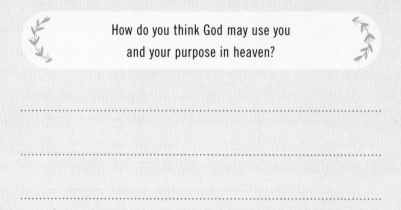

How do you think God may use you
and your purpose in heaven?

What will you be relieved to lay down when this life ends and the next begins?

THE WEEKLY FAITH PROJECT

This yearly faith journal features beautifully illustrated journaling pages that will help you discover more intimacy and joy in your spiritual life.

THE WEEKLY GRATITUDE PROJECT

The Weekly Gratitude Project is a 52-week guided gratitude journal that offers a life-changing journey through reflection prompts and inviting questions to guide you into a deeper relationship with God.

THE WEEKLY PRAYER PROJECT

Are you ready to accept a challenge that could change your life? *The Weekly Prayer Project* invites you to journal, pray, reflect, and connect with God using a 52-week guided prayer journal.

THE WEEKLY SELF-CARE PROJECT

Do you have a self-care action plan? Does your self-care routine need improvement? Equip yourself with the strategies and inspiration to take care of yourself—body, mind, and soul— with this 52-week guided journal.